DOCKSIDE

STAGE 1

BOOK 3

SWEET FEET

Philippa Bateman

RISING STARS

Can I see the TV?
HI!

No!

Eek! Keep your feet off.

My feet are sweet!

Dad! Tell JJ to keep his feet off.
TIMES

JJ. Keep your feet
off Tasha.

Dad! Tell him.

JJ. Your feet reek.

My feet are sweet!
HI!

They seem bad this week.

What's that?

It's a bee! Eek!
zzzzzzzzzzzzzzzzzzzz

ZZZZZZZZZZzzzzzzzzzzzzzzzz

I need to flee.
It's OK. The bee is off too.

It must be the reek of your feet, JJ. They are not sweet!